Why Go Green?

**It can be difficult to make changes in our lives.
For many, any potential change needs a good reason.**

In many parts of the world, human beings have a higher standard of living than has ever been seen before on this planet. The problem is, to maintain this standard we are using 25% more natural resources than our earth can possibly sustain. We can't go on like that forever.

Our energy consumption and industrial output are causing us to emit huge quantities of carbon dioxide and other dangerous greenhouse gases into the earth's atmosphere. This traps heat and ultimately causes climate change.

Climate change poses a great threat to the future of plants, humans and animals on this planet. Rising temperatures can result in decreased crop yields, rising ocean levels, increased rainfall and risk of flooding and wildfires.

Tip!

Earth Day is a great day to make a good choice! On Earth Day, we could either donate money to plant a tree, or plant a tree ourselves!

Dear Families!

Please join us as we travel through the world of ideas and issues surrounding the concept of sustainability!

Sustainability is a simple, yet big, idea. It means that we sustain ourselves on our wonderful, delicate planet without taking so much from it that it can't sustain its future inhabitants. To do that, we have to rethink many of our choices and take a look at what we consider important in life.

Think of it like the emergency instructions on airplanes that instruct parents to place the oxygen mask on themselves first before they assist their children. In this book, we are following the same idea. In the first part, we are going to look at what makes us happy and fulfilled as human beings. In the second part, we will look at what we can do to save our planet. Because car-

ing for ourselves empowers us to care for our planet. Knowing what is good for us, translates into knowing what is good for our environment.

Throughout this book you will find explanations of ideas and concepts, fun facts, as well as green lifestyle tips and suggestions for arts and crafts activities. It is meant to be an easy reference book, something you don't necessarily have to read through from beginning to end. We hope you will drop in often, and that from each reading you will take away a new idea, a new fact, and even a new action plan for yourself.

We are really excited that you have decided to travel with us!

List of contents

Go Green – A Family Guide to a Sustainable Lifestyle
Inspired by Erin L. Thompson
© 2014 Disney Enterprises, Inc. all rights reserved.
Illustrations © Magnus B. Oskarsson
Authors: Asthildur Bjorg Jonsdottir, Ellen Gunnarsdottir,
Gunndis Yr Finnbogadottir
Editor: Tinna Proppe, tinna@eddausa.com
Layout and design: Magnus B. Oskarsson
Cover design: Gassi.is
Printing: Prentmidlun / Printed on FSC Certified paper
Distributed by Midpoint Book Sales & Distribution

ISBN 978-1-94078-700-8
www.eddausa.com

GO GREEN!

A Family Guide to a
Sustainable Lifestyle

EDDA

Edda Publishing Usa LLC

Lifelong Curiosity

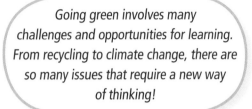

Going green involves many challenges and opportunities for learning. From recycling to climate change, there are so many issues that require a new way of thinking!

Keeping an open mind for new opportunities for learning is an important part of making our lives sustainable. Learning how to be sustainable is a lifelong process. So long as we're ready to learn, there's always more knowledge to be gained!

To learn new skills we need to practice. To learn to dance we need to practice dancing. To learn to live we need to practice living. It's the same principle. If we keep practicing the art of living we'll learn to make conscious decisions about how we act.

Sometimes we need to push ourselves to learn new things. Finding what really lies at the outer reaches of our abilities can be a great learning curve.

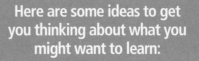

Here are some ideas to get you thinking about what you might want to learn:

Learn how to grow vegetables in a container.

Figure out how to do something new with a computer or smart-phone.

Inquire about your family history by learning how to trace your ancestry.

Join a club and learn how to play a new sport.

Join a choir and extend your skills in singing.

Learn how to play the harmonica, penny whistle or another musical instrument.

Learn how to knit, crochet or sew, and give what you make to friends or family members.

Try out some new cooking recipes.

Take up bird watching or star gazing.

Did you know?

✿ *That every year our daily activities release more than 30 billion tons of carbon dioxide into the atmosphere? It's way more than it can take!*

✿ *That we are currently experiencing the fastest rates of extinction for animals and plants since the days of the dinosaurs?*

✿ *That the decade between 2000 and 2010 was the warmest on record?*

✿ *That if we turn off the water while we brush our teeth, we can save eight gallons of water every day?*

✿ *That manufacturing one plastic water bottle uses more water than is actually put in the bottle? Making plastic also emits a lot of toxins in the air, and it takes hundreds of years to break down.*

This book helps people to understand what it means to live green! So they can answer the big question:

WHY GO GREEN?

When we decide to try and change our lifestyle, it's important to find our own reasons for why! We can ask ourselves simple questions like:

- What do I eat and how do I select my choices?

- How and why do I go to school or work?

- Why do I pay my bills?

One reason we do things is that there are consequences when we do not do them! So it can be good to think about the consequences of not Going Green! To do this we need to examine the big picture.

Everything we do, every day, has an impact on the planet. Some of it is good, some not so good and some of it is bad. Most often we have the power to control our individual choices. This is why we can also control the impact we have on the planet.

Well-being With Mickey

Natural environment
Resource conservation
Sustainable food production
Happiness
Population density
Health & wellness
Ecological Footprint
Recreation & leisure
Public and private infrastructure
Employment
Affordable goverment
Time-use
Affordable housing
Education
Living standards
Ethnic diversity
Economic vitality
Trust & belonging
Citizenship
Safety & crime
Community vitality
Equity & fairness

We have to remember that no one can give us well-being. We have to take action for ourselves.

way that is good for you is also good for those around you, and, in a larger sense, good for our planet.

Well-being can take many different forms, but a useful description is feeling good and functioning well. If we feel content and confident we are able to enjoy and

When we talk about well-being, we mean more than just happiness. It means we take care of every part of ourselves, both mind and body. We see them, as a whole, connected to the larger world. Living in a

engage with the world. This helps us develop self-esteem.

However, reaching a balance between ecology and well-being can sometimes be difficult. Sometimes, we make wrong decisions, but it is very important to never give up.

It is important to learn to think of our own well-being as part and parcel of the earth's well-being. This way we are more likely to live a happy life.

But we should always remember that opinions about what makes for a good life are different among individuals, and between different societies and cultures.

Establishing goals for a sustainable life is a very personal process. It wouldn't necessarily work to take ideas about what is a good life in one culture and apply it to another.

A big part of well-being is having a healthy sense of self and being able to look at one's actions from the outside, and even to criticize them.

Try looking at things that we often neglect, such as:

❁ The way light shines on water, or the way wind makes ripples in the grass.

❁ The detail of a butterfly's wings, a bird soaring overhead, or an animal walking by.

❁ All these ideas offer us a chance to see things that we often take for granted, in a new way.

Think about what you have done in the past to achieve well-being, and whether it worked. Then think about new things to try.

Tip!

It helps to take time to reflect on what makes you feel good and confident. Because focusing on the 'here-and-now' could make life more enjoyable. It also helps you to understand yourself more.

The Circle of Life

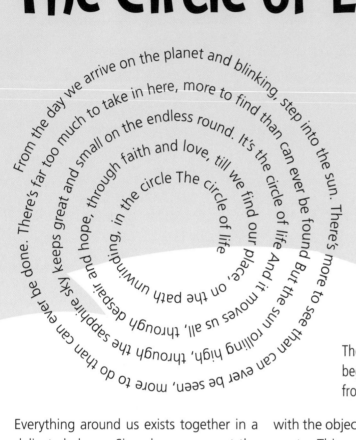

From the day we arrive on the planet and blinking, step into the sun. There's more to see than can ever be seen, more to do than can ever be done. There's far too much to take in here, more to find than can ever be found But the sun rolling high, through the sapphire sky keeps great and small on the endless round. It's the circle of life And it moves us all, through despair and hope, through faith and love, till we find our place, on the path unwinding, in the circle The circle of life

The Lion King's circular narrative begins – 'The Circle of Life`, from Disney's The Lion King

Everything around us exists together in a delicate balance. Since humans are at the top of the food chain, it is important that we understand the balance between nature and ourselves. We need to respect all life forms around us from the tiniest insect to the tallest tree.

All living things depend on one another and all life can be impacted by the smallest changes in the environment. Humans can affect nature in many different ways. This is why it is so important for us to create a system where we produce as little waste as possible. The waste we create

with the objects we make is called product waste. This waste could possibly be used somewhere else to create less waste.

If we want the earth to survive, now is the time to start caring for it. If we become responsible caretakers of our planet now, we ensure the well-being of future generations. Let's consider the life of our planet as a gift, or a resource to be used with care. Organic life on this earth moves in a sacred circle. For too long now, humans have viewed it as a process that goes in one direction only, that is to satisfy human demands.

Composting may not save the world, or preserve life on this planet single-handedly. But in our 'throw away society` it's one more way to support the circle of life and the perpetual return to beginnings.

Connect With Others

> *Connecting with other people is one of the cornerstones of our lives.*

Connecting with the people around us makes us feel good, like we are part of a family, a group of friends, a workplace, or a classroom. Wherever we connect with people, we are building a sense of community. We share our stories and our experiences. We are all in this life on earth together!

It can be fun to connect with people in new and unexpected places. Sometimes everybody is just waiting for one person to start connecting, and then everyone is doing it!

- Strengthen your relationship with people who are close to you.

- Each day make time to spend with your family and do something special together.

- Arrange to see friends that you haven't seen for a while.

- Switch off the TV and play a game or just talk.

- Speak to someone you have never spoken to before and broaden your connection to the wider community.

- Visit a friend or family member who needs support or company.

- Join an after-school activity or a volunteer organization.

It can be great fun to invite friends over for a scavenger hunt.

Divide the guests into teams. Each team has to have a digital camera which they will use to take pictures of natural elements, depending on the season.

You can also play this game in the car if you are going on a holiday. Give each child a list of items to watch for while driving. The list can be created ahead of time and adjusted to the places you are going to visit. For example, if you're going to be traveling in the desert, you will want to add items like a cactus, tumbleweed, wind turbine, etc. Once you have reached your destination, you can talk about the photographs.

No Man is an Island

We make meaningful connections in school, when playing sports or music, in church, during summer camp, in the scouts, and in our after-school activities. But we can also make great connections with people when we go to the shop, to farmers' markets, farmstands, harvest fairs or volunteer days at a neighbouring farm, or join in celebrations such as Earth Day. Garage sales, stoop sales, fund drives and all types of volunteer activities are also fun ways to connect with people you might not know from your immediate environment.

Did you know?

That the phrase 'No man is an island', comes from English poet John Donne who lived four centuries ago. People have been considering the benefits of connecting with others for a long time!

Sometimes you can tell a good joke to connect to other people.

What did the snowman say to the other snowman?

Can you smell carrots?

What do fireflies say when they are about to start a race?

On your marks! Get set! Glow!!!!!

What did the mother bee say to the baby bee?

Beehive yourself!

Nurturing relationships you have with other people can help you feel happier and more secure. It can give you a greater sense of purpose!

Even when you're really busy try to make time for your friends!

Did you know?

That some researchers suggest that connecting with others is as beneficial to our health as exercise and eating well. It can lower our stress levels and improve our heart rate!

Be Active

Our bodies are made to be active. Being active makes us feel good as it releases endorphins to our brains. As we go through our day, we do many things that make our bodies feel good. We walk or run, we play games, ride a bicycle, or dance. There are endless possibilities for strengthening our bodies, making them more flexible, and our minds more comfortable and at ease.

Sometimes making green choices takes us out of our comfort zone. It takes us away from the things we usually do and what's comfortable for us. At these times, it's good to remember that we're doing what's best for us, and what's best for the environment.

Being active can also improve your mental well-being because your mind and body are not separate.

What you do with your body can have a powerful effect on feeling good - both about yourself and about the world around you.

Being active builds physical health and fitness.

Everyone has their own favorite thing that they like to do. You might want to draw up a list of what you like to do. You could even make a list of activities that you haven't tried yet but would like to. Trying new things can help you find the kind of activity that best fits with who you are.

Don't forget about our winged friends during cold seasons. Make them a treat!

Mix water with gelatin powder in your bowl and stir until the gelatin powder dissolves completely. Add two cups of birdseed to the gelatin mix. Stir until all the birdseed is completely coated. If, after thorough stirring, there's a still a pool of gelatin at the bottom of the bowl, add a bit more birdseed. Spread a sheet of wax or parchment paper on a cookie sheet and

place your cookie cutters on top. Start filling the cookie cutters with your birdseed mixture until you fill half the cookie cutter. Cut a piece of twine and lay the two loose ends onto the seed mix so that a loop forms at the top and hangs off of the side. Continue to fill the cookie cutter with your seed mixture until the cookie cutter is completely full. Use your fingers, or a utensil to tamp down the seed. Place your feeders (still on the cookie tray) in a spot where they can sit overnight to dry; turn them over a couple of times to help them dry thoroughly. When your bird treats are dry, push them (carefully!) out of the cookie cutters. Hang them outside and wait for your feathered friends to arrive.

The Great Outdoors

Exploring the outdoors is a great way to be active. Hiking and walking, exploring nature and admiring its wonders, are ways to achieve sustainable happiness. What is sustainable happiness? It's the kind of happiness that doesn't come from acquiring new possessions, but from doing things that do not harm the earth.

Minnie Mouse and Mickey Mouse love to do things together, but some days they are not sure of what to do. They made a list of all the activities that they like to do, or want to try. On their list are many activities that are fun, free, and don't cost the earth anything!

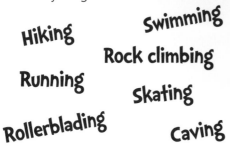

Hiking

Swimming

Rock climbing

Running

Skating

Rollerblading

Caving

You have to be active to achieve your dreams. Perhaps you have dreams that you have yet to accomplish. Most people do. One reason dreams sometimes don't come true is that it's hard work to attain them. It helps to set milestones on your journey to reach your dreams. You can write down specific action steps to take towards attaining your goals. Then you might set aside a few hours a week to actually take the steps. Make sure you have set a realistic time frame to complete each step!

It's fun to make your own dream catchers! You can make different designs and use all different types of materials. The hoop is the base for your catcher and the rest is up to you. You can choose colorful strings and even add natural materials too!

Physical activity helps kids be fit and healthy in all sorts of ways, such as:

- ❋ *Maintaining a healthy weight.*
- ❋ *Having strong bones and muscles.*
- ❋ *Improving balance and flexibility.*
- ❋ *Bettering posture.*
- ❋ *Preserving a healthy heart and blood vessels.*
- ❋ *Preventing disease later in life.*
- ❋ *Helping them relax.*
- ❋ *Developing stronger self-esteem.*
- ❋ *Cultivating social skills and making friends.*

Did you know?

People with higher levels of physical activity are at lower risk for developing chronic disease.

Be Curious,
Notice New Things

The world around us is full of beautiful and surprising things. We run across hundreds of them in the course of an ordinary day. All we have to do is to decide that we are going to start paying attention to what we see and feel. We might start looking for unusual sights and sounds in our environment that we have never noticed before.

Sharing your experience with your family in the evening is a great way to be mindful of the new things you tried, saw or experienced!

Perhaps you just noticed what the ground felt like under your feet as you walked to school.

Or what your sandwich tasted like during lunch.

Or a new word your friend used in conversation.

It can be fun to keep a journal of all the new things you notice in the course of your day!

Did you know?

That walking like a fox in the woods is a great way to experience your surroundings! A fox treads carefully on the ground, making sure he doesn't snap any twigs under his paws in case it's on the hunt. Walking like a fox involves moving slowly, putting your heel down first, then the sides of your foot, then your toes. Try it out with a blindfold when you're with a friend for added fun.

Notice How the Seasons Change

> *To celebrate the rhythms of the seasons, we might do some arts and crafts activities.*

We all notice when the seasons change. In the autumn, forests turn yellow, red, purple and orange. The leaves fall to create a thick blanket on the ground and the air grows cooler. Small forest creatures are busy hoarding their food for the winter.

Winter brings short days and long nights. Some days are beautiful and still, others are dramatic and loud.

Spring brings the forest back to its green color and the animals begin to bring their young ones into the world.

In summer, nature is so alive and busy that it takes our breath away.

In every season, nature is brimming with things to pay attention to: twigs, pine-cones, vines, flowers, leaves, rocks, shells, moss, small creatures and large. Every detail comes in so many forms and shapes!

In autumn, for example, we can make leaf banners and crowns, do wheat weaving and make lanterns.

In winter, we can care for the birds and squirrels. We can make star windows and snow scenes, do finger knitting and make yarn dolls.

In spring, we can make round wind wands, dish gardens, butterfly pop-up cards, May baskets or pressed flower cards.

In summer, we can make shooting star streamer balls, walnut boats, parachute people, paper birds and make moving pictures.

Keep Learning

Learning never ends, it goes on our whole lives. Every time we try something new we are learning, discovering new knowledge or acquiring new skills. You don't have to be in the classroom to learn something new: your neighborhood, town or city, your country, and the whole world is your classroom.

Your parents can also learn a lot from what you are doing. They might try to learn to play the instrument you're learning to play. They might try ice skating, or learning the new language you are learning in school. We all learn from one another!

Deciding that you want to try a new activity every day is a great way to keep learning. You might want to try a new type of food, or a different outdoor or indoor activity, It doesn't have to be a big thing, the small things are just as important.

Make a list of all the new things you've been trying lately. Perhaps you will soon find that it includes wonderful new discoveries!

Learning how to make new things from old is a big part of going green!

If you are already reading this book, it means that you are curious and ready to try new things!

Giving

Good friends make us feel so special!

Good friends are always showing us how much they care!

It feels good to give. Sometimes we just have to learn to enjoy giving to realize how fulfilling it is. We can practice giving every day. It doesn't have to be a big thing: smiling or giving a few minutes of your time, holding the door open for others, greeting people nicely in the morning; these are all examples of giving.

When we think about giving, it's also important to look inside ourselves. What makes us happy? Is it possible that what makes me happy also makes the person next to me happy? This is a way to both learn more about yourself, and learn how to put yourself in other people's shoes.

Smile!

Open the door for others!

Ask yourself: Am I a giving person?

It can be fun to discuss with family and friends what it is that other people do for them that makes them happy. And what kind of giving they find rewarding. You can also make lists and compare them.

Even the smallest act can count, whether it's a smile, a thank you, or a kind word. Larger acts, such as volunteering at your local community center, can be very fulfilling.

Value Giving

Some people can be called ´a giving person`. But what does that mean?

• It means they go out of their way to make others' lives better, without expecting anything in return.

• It means they help those out who are less fortunate than themselves.

• It means they cut negativity out of their life and stay positive.

•It means they take others under their wing and help them get better at what they do well.

When you communicate with another person really think about whether or not you are making a positive or negative contribution to their life. Don't worry about what you stand to get in return. If you go through life contributing more value than you take, the world will start to reward you for it. People are drawn to value givers. Their attitudes are contagious!

Gifts For the Planet

Giving has so many different aspects. You might give birthday and Christmas presents to family and friends. But you might also go to the recycling center with your parents and leave the things you no longer use, for other people who might enjoy, or need them. Giving to people you don't know is just as rewarding as giving presents to friends and family. And when you recycle, you're giving a big gift to your community and to the planet.

People are always giving to one another. They might share seeds from their garden with neighbors or pass them around through seed-sharing clubs. They'll bring produce from their garden to friends' houses. If they are very good at making something, like honey from their bees or candles from beeswax, they'll give it to their friends, and that makes them feel good.

> *I feel grateful for my family and friends. I also feel very grateful to the earth because each day it gives me what I need to sustain myself!*

Did you know?

When you think of what makes you happy, take the time to be grateful for it. Feeling and showing gratitude increases our happiness.

Did you know?

Sustainability is about giving to the earth as much as you receive from it!

Did you know?

You can use recycled newspapers to wrap presents for your friends and family.

Making Good Choices

Values like respect, kindness, honesty, courage, perseverance, self-discipline, compassion, generosity, and dependability are some of the principles that help us live a good life. They guide us through many complicated situations and help us make good choices. Morals are about judging our actions based on our principles. They help us define what is a good action and what is bad.

Learning about values takes time and is often learned from others. It is important to talk about what is right and wrong, and what constitutes good behavior and what doesn't. When families have conversations about values on a regular basis, the topic becomes completely 'normal' in your household. The bottom line is that families need to communicate, to talk about what they did right, what they did wrong, and how to make better moral decisions.

> Treating others with love and respect sets a good example for everybody.

Did you know?

Being mindful of our values is especially important when going green! Because going green involves making a lot of responsible, and often difficult, choices every day!

When our values and morals help us live a good life, we feel a sense of self-esteem and pride. And when we feel like that, we are more likely to make good life choices. It all goes together!

When you start reading this chapter, you might want to make a list of values that help you make decisions and respond to situations that come up in school or at home. You also might want to make a list of moral judgements that you have made. If you think about it, you're always making moral judgements. It's a part of life.

This book is meant to help you develop your values, and perhaps rethink them.

We all need to rethink our values so that we can live within the limits of the earth's resources.

We all have habits. Some are good and some are bad. Good habits can be developed and bad ones broken, but it all takes effort!

Sit with your family around a table. Ask everyone to fold arms. Look who crosses the right arm over the left, and who crosses the left arm over the right. Most of the time it is even. Put your arms down and try to fold your arms the opposite way. It's difficult isn't it? It's hard to change old habits!!

Choosing Change

> *When you observe friends or family doing something good, make sure you tell them how great they are!*

Did you know?

Renewable energy supplies only 17% of the world's primary energy. This includes harnessing sources like biomass, including virgin wood, food and industrial waste, hydropower, wind, solar power, geothermal power, and bio fuels.

We all have our habits, certain ways of looking at things and thinking about them. But what if we were to change our views, switch sides and see the same thing from a new perspective? It might help us better understand when someone has an opposing opinion from ours.

Not everybody has the same idea about what constitutes sustainability. Keeping that in mind helps us compromise and come to an agreement so that we can all focus on the important job of helping our planet stay healthy!

Did you know?

Many scientists are convinced that global warming is a fact. Global warming is the increase of the earth's average surface temperature due to greenhouse gases, such as carbon dioxide emissions from burning fossil fuels or from deforestation. These trap the heat that would otherwise escape from Earth.

Almost every day something happens that can provide families with an opportunity to talk about, or work with, their values. You could, for example, create a collage from news headlines that interest you. Or work with the images to find connections between your actions and beliefs.

Tip!

Families can create a platform to talk about mistakes. They can discuss potential role models for a sustainable lifestyle. They could be fictional characters or people you know.

We often make mistakes on the road to going green. If we're tolerant of our own mistakes, and those of others, we can learn from them and do positive things for the earth!

Some people may think sustainability is only about recycling, others may think it's only about turning off the lights when leaving a room. These are important ideas, but sustainable development is an endless journey.

to utilize the clearly visible power of water and wind for driving machinery.

Consequences of global warming include drought, severe hurricanes, massive fires, and melting of the polar caps.

We all make mistakes, and when we are young, we are more likely to get ourselves into trouble. We might break the neighbor's window while playing baseball, perform poorly on the job, get fired, or disobey school rules. It is important to be accountable for our mistakes so that we can learn from them.

Renewable energy sources have been important for humans since the beginning of civilization. Biomass has been used for centuries for heating and cooking. For a long time now mankind has known how

Truth

On a day off it's nice to curl up on the sofa and watch a favorite TV show. But perhaps you've volunteered to join friends who are cleaning up trash on the riverbank near town. It's best to keep that promise!

Getting into the habit of always speaking the truth is a good idea. It makes us feel good. We begin to trust ourselves more and that gives others a reason to trust us. Trust builds relationships and communities. Eventually, if we trust one another, it's easier to build a sustainable future. When we are honest with other people it's also easier to find out what's in our own minds and hearts. It helps us build knowledge of ourselves.

If kids hear adults tell their boss that they're sick when they don't want to go to work, kids won't think there's anything wrong with lying. The same is true if an adult asks a child to answer the phone and say that they're not at home.

Did you know?

If adults want kids to exhibit values like honesty, self-respect and compassion, they need to show these qualities themselves. All the teaching in the world can be undone if kids watch adults behave in ways that contradict what they have said.

Did you know?

When it comes to honesty we're all role models for one another. Parents are role models for their kids and kids are role models for their parents. Friends are role models for friends and strangers can be role models for strangers.

I'm going to try to remember to acknowledge my mistake if I fall short with someone. But it's not enough to just acknowledge my mistake. I also need to tell them that I'm sorry. I respect others and take responsibility for my mistakes.

Right conduct

Right conduct is a way to live your life without hurting others. There are so many things that we can do to live in peace and harmony with all creatures. Good manners and respect for others is one way. Being responsible and controlling one's impulses is another. Showing courage in a difficult situation helps everyone around you. And knowing where your duty lies and understanding where you can be of service to other people greatly improves the lives of the people in your community.

Love

You can also get involved in a more formal type of service project. It might include visiting nursing homes, helping the local food bank collect donations of canned goods, or getting involved in a community service organization.

Love is what keeps our families, our circles of friends and our larger communities going. When people experience caring, kindness and empathy from another person, they are more likely to give those same qualities to others. If we can show compassion, forgiveness, empathy and acceptance, the whole world is more likely to live in peace forever.

Tip!

If you read an article in the newspaper about someone's heroic deed, you might talk to friends about what you would have done if you had been in the same situation.

Non-violence

When we spread love around the world, a great many wonderful things happen. We begin to co-operate rather than argue, we give everybody a fair go, we respect our fellow creatures, and we respect our earth. Citizenship is about doing all these things, and about including everybody in an equal manner.

The International Day of Non-Violence is marked on October 2nd, the birthday of Mahatma Gandhi, the late leader of the Indian independence movement and pioneer of the philosophy and strategy

If you never take more from the earth than you need to sustain yourself, you're less likely to get into quarrels with others over things you want.

If ypu get angry or disappointed, try pausing for a moment after the impulse, before taking action. That way you never say anything you would later regret.

Say you win five boxes of chocolates at the school lottery. You with a friend divide them between you but that leaves one box out. Since you know you don't need more than two boxes to sustain yourself, you could give up the third!

of non-violence. He once said: 'There are many causes that I am prepared to die for but no causes that I am prepared to kill for.' Try to discover the richness of empathy. Be inspired, contribute to others, express yourself, just listen, or ask for empathy.

Did you know?

Sincere praise goes a long way in reinforcing behaviors you'd like to see more of?

Peace

This is the internationally recognized symbol for peace, which was originally designed in 1958 by Gerald Holtom.

The symbol is a combination of the semaphore signals for the letters N and D, standing for 'nuclear disarmament.'

Each and every one of us can work for peace in the world simply by doing our best in our daily lives. If you are calm, patient and content, it is more likely that people around you will be calm, patient and content, and that good feeling is then returned. The same goes when you have confidence and respect for yourself. It provides a good model for other people. When we are peaceful, we are able to better concentrate. And when we put all those things together, we are creating more space, and more freedom for ourselves as individuals.

Did you know?

A safe and comfortable home environment is created when family members communicate with one another. State your opinions openly and encourage kindness by being kind.

Cultivating a plot in a community garden actually contributes to world peace? Every little action counts!

Each year the International Day of Peace is observed around the world on September 21st. It is a good day to focus on the value of tolerance and mutual respect. Peaceful people are fair and embrace diversity.

Tip!

Look for community projects in your neighborhood. Every time people come together for a common purpose, a new opportunity for more peace in the world is created!

What is peace?

- *Peace is more than the absence of war.*
- *Peace is living in harmony and not fighting with others.*
- *If everyone in the world were peaceful, this would be a peaceful world.*
- *Peace is being quiet.*
- *Peace is a calm and relaxed state of mind.*
- *Peace consists of positive thoughts, pure feelings, and good wishes.*
- *Peace begins within each one of us.*
- *To stay peaceful requires strength and compassion.*
- *Peace is a qualitative energy that brings balance.*
- *World peace grows through non-violence, acceptance, fairness and communication.*
- *Peace is the main characteristic of a civilized society.*
- *Peace must begin with each one of us. Through quiet and serious reflection, new and creative ways can be found to foster understanding, friendship and cooperation*

What is an Ecological Footprint?

> How big
> is your footprint ?

We leave our footprints in the sand, in the mud, and even in our house when our shoes are dirty. The footprint we leave on the planet is called an ecological footprint. We can't see it with our bare eyes but it's there and it has a huge impact on our planet.

An ecological footprint is a measure of how much we take from the earth's resources to produce all the things we need and use in our daily lives.

The choices we make determine the size of our footprint. Our common goal should be to make the necessary changes to leave as small a footprint as possible!

Your ecological footprint tells you how much farmland, grazing land, forest and fishing grounds are needed to produce your food, goods, services, housing, and energy, and how much it takes to dispose of your waste.

There are many websites that allow you to calculate your footprint, and the outcome tells you how many planets we would need if everyone lived their lives like you do.

Your ecological footprint is determined by four different footprints. Their names tell us which parts of our lives they refer to:

* *Carbon footprint*
* *Food footprint*
* *Housing footprint*
* *Goods and services footprint*

Activity!

Calculate your ecological footprint with your family. Make a list of things you could do to reduce your footprint, and what is essential to keep. You might discover that you could easily save a lot of water in your home, but you still need to drive to visit your grandma.

Carbon Footprint

Our planet breathes. It inhales carbon dioxide and stores it in forests and oceans, leaves and soil. But when we burn fossil fuels and drill for oil, the earth exhales carbon dioxide in such quantities that plants and trees are overwhelmed. They can't absorb it back up.

All the land and water needed to store the carbon emissions released by our individual energy use is what makes our carbon footprint.

Responsibility for reducing our carbon footprint lies with each and every one of us. The most effective way to do this is to rethink our daily routines and habits.

Did you know?

That every hour the sun beams onto the earth, it produces enough energy to satisfy global energy needs for an entire year?

Tip!

If you're committed to change there are so many small things you can do to raise awareness! Discuss your concerns with your family or, if the situation is appropriate, bring them up when you run into neighbors and friends on the street.

Keep in mind:

- Save electricity. Forgetting to flip the light switch or turn off electrical appliances after you have used them adds to your carbon footprint, as does leaving the lights on in the house when you leave.

- Driving your car to the store and to your friend's house, to birthday parties and sports classes, adds to your carbon footprint. If you're not going too far, try to convince your parents to walk with you, instead of taking the car.

Try to use public transportation as much as possible instead of your private car.

It saves gas to ride with public transportation, and it pollutes much less if there are fewer private cars on the street. Also, it is much cheaper to take the bus than your own car, but if you must drive, try to carpool if possible.

By making good choices in our daily lives, we're already helping our planet breathe. But we can also advocate for change by getting the message out in our community. When communities come together as one they push local authorities to make sustainable decisions. It might be as simple as putting more buses on the road to make public transportation more efficient!

Tips for reducing your carbon footprint:

❀ Reduce. Reuse. Recycle.

❀ Recycle old electronic devices.

❀ Stop your junk mail.

❀ Buy locally if possible.

❀ Eat more vegetarian meals.

❀ Don't waste.

❀ Save water, take a short shower instead of a bath.

❀ Make sure to use energy-saving light bulbs, which save more than $2/3$ of the energy a regular one uses.

❀ Maintain your home's cooling and heating systems and make sure you are not overheating or cooling excessively.

❀ Buy ENERGY STAR appliances for your home.

❀ Try turning off the water when brushing your teeth. You can save thousands of gallons of water every year.

❀ Insulating your home saves energy, makes it more comfortable and helps you save money.

❀ Try alternative energy sources such as solar energy.

❀ Bigger is not always better! Get the fridge size you need, or the couch size you need.

Food Footprint

Your Food Footprint is the amount of farmland, grazing land, forest and fishing grounds needed to produce your food, plus all land and water needed to absorb the carbon emissions from the production and transportation of your food. The good news is that vegetables and fruits are very footprint friendly, and buying those that are grown close to your home is a way to shrink your footprint!

Did you know?

Did you know that a big portion of our footprint is the food we waste? This happens because we often buy more than we can eat, and it goes bad in our fridge. When you want a snack, don't go for the freshest looking banana. Go for the one that's turning a little brown. It's also much sweeter!

Good food is precious! If you can't finish yours, compost it to grow more precious food!

We could save energy by cooking fewer big meals. It reduces our footprint and saves money. But the biggest part of our food footprint has to do with how our food is made. This means that we have to make good choices when we buy our food, sourcing locally grown food whenever we can. Changing our diet is an effective way to shrink our food footprint. Growing some of our food ourselves, and using our own compost is a great and rewarding way to achieve a smaller footprint.

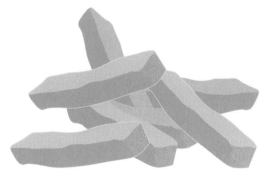

Tips to reduce your food footprint:

- Compost all, or most, of your food waste. If you're not ready to use the compost yourself, many cities and towns have compost collection programs. Garbage that doesn't include food waste is easier to recycle and sort.

- Change your diet. Eat a vegetarian meal at least one day a week.

- Reduce your use of disposable bags and plastic bags and bottles.

- Buy directly from local farmers or farmers markets.

- Grow your own food.

- Eat seasonally.

Make your own healthy chips!

Thinly slice root vegetables like potato, carrot, turnip, parsnip or sweet potato. Toss with oil or tamari sauce and spread in a single layer on a baking sheet. You can also use pieces of leafy veggies, like spinach or kale. Season to your liking with salt and pepper. Bake at 400° F, checking often for crispness.

Housing Footprint

Housing footprint includes the land your home sits on; the trees used for construction and furniture; water you and your family use in your home; and the land and sea that store the carbon emissions from constructing and maintaining your home.

When it comes to cleaning your house, it's important to keep your home and family safe by using non-toxic, all-natural alternatives to chemical cleaners.

Did you know?

Some houseplants can clean and filter the air naturally and inexpensively so you don't have to invest in expensive electrical air purifiers?

You can make a rag rug from old bed sheets. They add warmth to any room and last for a very long time. Plus, they are machine washable, becoming softer with each wash.

Tip!

Natural liquid dish soap makes a great bubble base. If you add a little sugar, corn syrup, or starch to the mixture, the bubbles become thicker and last longer. You can make a giant bubble wand from a wire coat hanger!

Tips to reduce your housing footprint!

❋ Choose secondhand, recycled or sustainably produced furniture.

❋ Use non-toxic, all natural, environmentally-friendly cleaning products.

❋ Plant trees in your yard, and grow vegetables and herbs in your garden, balcony or on your window.

❋ Don't wash your car too often. Take it to a carwash. Commercial carwashes use less water and should drain water into the sewage system, rather than into storm drains. This protects aquatic life.

Instead of getting your friend a new sports bag for her birthday, take her on an outdoor adventure course!

Goods and Services Footprint

Goods are items you buy like clothes, furniture and electronics. Goods require large amounts of energy, land and water to make and maintain. When energy is used to manufacture goods, carbon dioxide is released into the atmosphere. We know that excess carbon dioxide does not help our planet stay healthy!

Services include things that are not necessarily our personal choice. We don't always need them, but our community often does. They include hospitals, libraries, Internet and telephone service, schools, banks, businesses, and government agencies.

Since our lifestyles are increasingly dependent on goods and services, this category makes up a significant part of our overall footprint.

There are many things that we need and many things that make our lives better. But having a smaller ecological footprint means that we need to consume less. How do we decide what we need and what we don't? Before you make your decisions, consult with people you trust. Avoid rushing into buying new things. If you really want to buy a new computer game, take your time and think it through. You might find that your best friend has it, and you could borrow it and lend your friend your games in exchange. If you decide to buy it, try to get it secondhand or see if you could legally download it from the Internet. This reduces the amount of packaging material you would need to recycle.

Using fewer services will reduce your goods and services footprint, but it isn't always sensible. How can that be? Because if buying more service will result in spending less on housing, travel, food or products, then we are better off. Services are usually better for the environment. Luckily, running schools leaves a smaller footprint compared to the other footprints.

Using the money you would otherwise spend on a new toy or new clothes to buy tickets for a play or a movie is a greener choice. Having less stuff often results in more time and space for the activities you enjoy.

Keep in mind:

- **Using paper adds to your footprint. Why?**
- **First, it takes energy to harvest paper from a plant.**
- **Second, it takes energy for the plant to grow into a tree.**
- **Third, it takes energy to cut down the tree and transport it to a paper mill.**
- **Fourth, it takes energy and water to produce paper in the mill.**

So don't throw your books away! Give them away or recycle them!

We have seen that there are many simple things that we can do to quickly reduce our ecological footprint. Understanding the size of our ecological footprint is the first step!

Your ecological footprint matters because every single one of us has one!

Add to your impact by inspiring others to follow in your footsteps. Engage your family, friends and community to support local and global organizations that work to preserve our environment. Or start your own movement!

Look for certified fair-trade products. They support producers that focus on secure and sustainable livelihoods.

The Three R's of Sustainability

REDUCE   REUSE,   RECYCLE

These three simple words represent a very big concept. They are the key words of sustainability. Thinking of them as a circle helps us figure out what they really mean.

They all hang together. We could call them steps 1, 2, and 3. All of us can utilize these three steps. The first step is to reduce what we use and consume. The second is to make sure that what we buy can be reused at a later date. The third step is to recycle everything we cannot reuse. The outcome is that we keep our carbon footprint as small as possible. If we all practice the three R's, we move away from a mindset that views the planet as one great resource that we're all entitled to use, to being responsible caretakers of our environment.

Activity!

If taking out the trash is one of your chores, you know how big a full trash bin is. Calculate how many bins you go through in a month; then calculate how many households there are in your building or street. Add it all up and you can imagine the amount of trash that goes weekly into a landfill from your neighborhood!

Maybe it's not necessary
to buy three pairs of shorts,
even if they're on sale.

That old shoebox
you never used for your pencils
could be recycled.

That yellow dress still
hanging in the closet could go
to the thrift shop

Did you know?

Circular currents in the Pacific and Atlantic oceans have generated gigantic patches of marine debris, mostly made up of plastics. In one square mile of the Great Pacific Garbage Patch, scientists have collected 1.9 million waste bits! They pose a great danger to all forms of life in the sea.

Reduce

It's great that we're all recycling! But we can do even more to keep our planet safe for the future by reducing our waste even before we recycle. All this requires that we rethink our choices. One way to figure it out is to ask yourself some simple questions when you go to the store:

Do I really need this?

How will I use it?

How much of it do I really need?

How was it made? What is the lifecycle of this product?

Did you know that biodegradable bags are made from corn and wheat starch?

Tip!

Buying fresh fruits and vegetables at the store instead of pre-packaged or canned vegetables reduce our waste significantly!

Did you know that plastic bags are not biodegradable? They break down into smaller particles that contaminate the ground and are very difficult to remove. And recycling them is not simple. Only about one-tenth of the plastic bags we use get recycled. So it's better not to use them at all.

Try cutting up scrap paper to make origami sheets. You might end up with a really interesting collection!

Look around your house. Try to imagine which of the objects around you can be recycled. If there's an item you're not sure about, try looking it up on the Internet.

Go for a litter walk! Take a large bag with you, and pick up whatever you find on the street that isn't too yucky! Recycle whatever you can, and throw out the rest. You'll see that the strangest things get thrown on the street!

Reduce

Old curtains bought at the thrift store could make a nice Ancient Egyptian costume!

Tip!

Always write or draw on both sides of your paper. This can reduce the amount of paper we recycle by half!

Tip!

If you need new bookshelves for your room ask around for old wooden crates used to carry fruit and vegetables. Once stacked up they make nice deep shelves. And they're easy to move around!

When you go to the supermarket, notice how products are packaged. Small, individually packaged items take more energy to produce and they leave more waste. Snack items that we take to school or work often come in small sizes.

Sometimes we need things we only use once or twice, like a costume for a school play or a Halloween party. Or a book we need to read for school. Consider borrowing from a friend or buying it second hand. That way it's guaranteed that none of the earth's resources have gone into making something you only use once!

> *If you buy a large box of raisins and pour the amount you want into a reusable snack box for your lunch bag! You'll save both money and resources.*

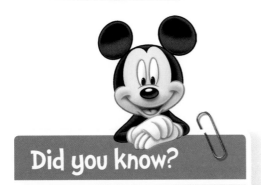

Tip!

Rather than buy twelve small juice boxes, buy a large box of juice and each day pour as much as you use into a reusable bottle.

Tip!

Works of art have a timeless value. If you want to redecorate your room, consider hanging up artwork by yourself, friends and family. They don't cost the earth anything and they will add a happy twist to your room!

Did you know?

That if all Americans recycled all their paper it would amount to 250 million trees a year?

It only takes two months to recycle an aluminium can and get it back on the shop shelf?

We can keep recycling glass almost forever. It takes 40 centuries for glass to break down!

Make sure you remember to reduce and re-use first, so that you don't have to recycle!

Did you know?

That we didn't invent recycling? Archaeological data shows that human beings have been recycling all kinds of objects for thousands of years!

That recycling plants use powerful magnets to sort metals of different kinds?

Did you know?

That garbage is a relatively new phenomenon? It was created when the world became industrialized.

Reuse

Finding a new purpose for old stuff you're thinking about throwing out can be a lot of fun! You can either pass it on to others or reuse it yourself, instead of letting it end up in a landfill. The environment will thank you for it.

Old kitchen chairs can get a new life with a bit of leftover paint.

An orange juice carton can turn into a bird feeder!

Did you know?

- That the rubber from old tires can be used to pave roads? And to make yoga mats?

- A jar of applesauce can become a great pencil holder?

- An empty bucket of paint can be used as a planter?

- That leftover Halloween candy can be turned into all kinds of fun little creatures? You just need candy, a toothpick and your creativity!

What about all that old stuff we don't have time to reuse? The best thing we can do is to give it away so others could reuse it. Charities, volunteer organizations and development agencies are all brilliant at finding new uses for old things. Use your possessions carefully, keeping in mind that others could use it once you're done with it. If you take the time to bring your old stuff to the right place, it will most probably end up in the hands of those who need it the most!

Thrift stores that are run by charities serve a dual purpose: to sell used clothes in good condition at affordable prices, and to channel the profits where they are needed.

Other fun ways to pass your old stuff to the right people are through stoop sales, garage sales, yard sales and flea markets. You might meet a lot of people and exchange stories and jokes. It's a way of strengthening a sense of community.

Try cutting a notch into a paper towel tube. You've made a Lincoln log! Collect as many tubes as you would like, and soon you'll have a Lincoln log house!

Activity!

Old egg cartons make great Halloween bats! All you need is an egg carton, a pair of scissors, some black paint and a few googly eyes. Cut out three cups from the carton, cut bat wing patterns into two cups, paint everything black and glue googly eyes onto the middle cup. And there's your bat!

Reuse

> *Did you know that clothes that are no longer usable sometimes end up as rubberized playground coverings?*

Tip!

Help your family and friends to think of new uses for their old stuff. You might want to exchange toys, clothes and sports equipment. Objects that we once cherished and used deserve a new life with another owner!

Make festive decorations from old magazines and newspapers!

To make a Christmas tree, you will need something you can use as the trunk. You might want to try a wooden stake from the garden, a knitting needle or a wooden skewer. Attach it to a sturdy base, like a piece of scrap wood, clay or floral foam.

Cut your magazines in different sized squares. Start with the largest ones and keep making them smaller as you go, until you have 10-20 of each size. Stack the paper pieces onto the tree trunk and place an ornament on the top. Make different sizes, and you have a forest!

Tip!

Give your old books to younger kids. Or put them in a box on your stoop with a sticker announcing that they're free for all book lovers. Or, if you want to collect money for new books, put an honesty box next to the book box and sell your books at 50 cents apiece!

A tea mug bought at a yard sale might become your favorite! You can also make some new friends at yard sales!

If you want to change to a healthier diet, you don't have to throw away your old cookbooks and get new ones. Supplement ingredients with healthier choices.

1 cup white flour becomes 1 cup sifted spelt, buckwheat, cornmeal or rice flour.

1 cup sugar becomes ¾ cup cane sugar or ½ cup agave syrup.

1 cup margarine becomes 1 cup butter or ¾ cup sunflower, olive, or coconut oil.

To change any yeast recipe to a cream of tartar recipe, use a teaspoon of cream of tartar for each half cup of flour.

Recycle

If your school has a vending machine, look around to see if there are recycling bins for aluminium cans!

Waste thrown into landfills emits a dangerous greenhouse gas called methane. This is a gas known to contribute to global warming. Recycling is one way to fight global warming. It's the process by which old materials are made new.

Paper, for example, is easy to recycle. Once it has been collected from your recycling bin, it's taken to a recycling plant where it's separated according to type of paper. Then it's put through a process where soapy water is used to wash off any print or material that sticks to it. Afterwards,

Tip!

Make yourself the boss of recycling in your house. Look for objects to recycle that your family members may not have realized they can recycle. Helping your parents take the recycling to the local collection centre is a great way to see what other people are doing about their recycling. It may give you a great sense of accomplishment and pride!

it's put into a large barrel with water and turned into a thick paste we call 'slurry.' The slurry is then spread with a roller into large sheets. Once dried, it's cut up again and brought back to the store. And no new trees have to be cut down in the process!

Recycling clothes and furniture is a great way of helping your community. Whether it is your personal clothes or furniture you no longer need, these donations can make a great difference to an individual. There are many organizations that accept donations.

Did you know?

That recycling one aluminium can saves enough energy to let your TV run for two to three hours?

You can recycle different materials to make a marble run. Discover gravity and speed with an easy to make, and super fun to play with contraption.

Did you know?

That a large part of the waste created by schools is paper? Check out what's being done in your school to recycle paper!

Recycle

Did you know that for one ton of recycled paper, we save almost 400 gallons of oil, three cubic yards of landfill, and 17 trees!

By recycling paper, bottles, jars, aluminium cans, packaging and kitchen and toilet paper rolls, you're already doing a lot for the environment. But we can do even more by looking for recycled products when we go to the supermarket. Many brands of toilet paper and kitchen rolls, even paper plates and cups, are made from recycled paper.

Did you know?

That recycled plastic bottles could actually become a component in the fabric used to make polar fleece? And newspaper can sometimes end up as an ingredient in countertops?

Activity!

When you go to the supermarket, have fun looking for recycled products on the shelves. You might be surprised at the great variety of products that can be made from the recycling process.

Have a blast creating stilts made out of empty tomato cans! Puncture a can in opposite spots on each side. Drain it by blowing into one hole to force the sauce out of the other. Repeat with the second can. Wash both cans under running water to clean them, inside and out. Remove their labels and let them dry. Paint both the cans. For the handles, tape one end of a length of clothesline to a skewer. Push it through one hole and out the other, as shown. Have your child stand on the can, holding the ends of the line. Tie the line at hip level and trim. Repeat for the second stilt.

Some toys are even made out of recycled plastic or wood! Look for them the next time you go to the toy store!

Did you know?

- That when we recycle, compost, and reuse, we reduce our waste stream by up to 75%?

- You could even buy jeans made mostly from recycled materials!

Craft Cupboard

> *Old telephone wire is material for art.*

Waste materials can be resources for creation. It can be a lot of fun to make a craft cupboard in your home by collecting reclaimed materials. You could use stock paper, cardboard, ceramics, paints, cords, leather, rubber, wood, bottle caps, used sweaters and other odds and ends. These items can become your art scrap, waiting to be reinvented. Giving value to rejected materials, imperfect products, and otherwise worthless objects, fosters understanding of the environment.

When you store the things you have collected, it is important to organize the goods. Once you have found a useful storage space, you can organize the found elements by their nature, color, size, etc. You can use all kinds of objects such as old glass jars, yogurt cups, shoeboxes, small containers for salads, or other food containers.

It's great fun to make mandalas from your material. Take pictures of your mandalas and make them your greeting cards. Once you have worked with the mandala, you should store your material in the right place.

Tip!

Ask your friends and family to help you organize the materials you find. They might be able to help you with your creation.

Did you know?

You can make games with numbers and found materials and take turns to create something from found objects. See how many different images can be made from the same number of items!

1 piece of bark

2 feathers

3 small stones

4 (tiny) flowers

5 sticks as big as your pinky finger

6 leaves

7 something that no one else would find

Arts and Crafts Spring

In spring, when nature is waking up, take a walk in the woods, in the park or on the beach. Give yourself the time you need to explore shapes, colors and textures. Sometimes grownups are in such hurry, they don't give themselves enough time for making new discoveries. Spring is a great time to slow down and rediscover our environment. Gather natural materials to create a giant collage of an imaginary animal or creature. This way you can re-visit all the interesting shapes and colors you found.

As the ground thaws and the spring rains begin, try painting a vivid mural on a big rock. You can make your own paints from all kinds of natural materials you find on a scavenger hunt. These include clay, mud, roots, petals, leaves and soil paint.

How to make soil paint

You'll need:

Air-dried soil samples of different colors and textures

Re-sealable freezer bags

Rolling pin or similar tool, like a glass bottle

Sieves or meshes

Paper plates

Plastic cups

Sticks for stirring

Water

Paint brushes

Start by making a collection of different soils from around your school, your backyard, the park, or the woods. Remove grass, roots and bugs from your soil samples before you air-dry them. Put your dried soil in freezer bags. Move your rolling pin over the bag to break down lumps in the soil. Note on each sample where it came from.

Pour your soil through sieves onto a paper plate and discard what remains in the sieve. Pour the refined soil into a paper cup and add water until you have the consistency of whipped cream. You can add a drop of dishwashing liquid if the paint doesn't flow easily.

Arts and Crafts
Summer

Many plants have very strong natural color pigments, which are very interesting to work with. In the summer, when the flowers are in bloom, it's great fun to make flower petal stained glass. To do that, you stick flower petals, and leaves onto contact paper, then onto the window.

Place a colorful leaf or petal on top of a textured paper like watercolor paper or soft wood, and cover with a paper towel. Then hammer the colors onto the paper. You can make interesting images using different plants and compositions.

Make your own natural watercolors!

The easiest way to make rich, natural watercolors is by boiling the plant with water to release its natural dyes. There are many common plants that can be used to create all-natural watercolor paints.

Red onion peels: crimson red and burgundy

Pokeberries: deep red

Orange pekoe tea: brown

Black walnuts: black

Queen Anne's Lace: green

Marigolds: yellow

Goldenrod: lime green

Blueberries: blue

Cayenne pepper: rust red

Yellow onion peels: various hues of yellow and tan

Coffee beans: browns and tans

Dandelions: mossy greens

Tip!

Try using leaves, sticks, grass and pinecones as paintbrushes!

In summer, it's fun to paint on your stoop or the sidewalk with sponge brushes. The best thing is that it's temporary. The paint will rinse off with water.

Sidewalk paint:

1 part cornstarch

1 part water

Food coloring

Mix cornstarch and water together.

Add the food coloring!

Arts and Crafts
Fall

Fall offers so many opportunities for arts and crafts activities! Collect different shaped leaves and make leaf rubbings. Paint leaf outlines or make a stamp with a leaf, or simply arrange the leaves by color or size.

In fall, you can find a treasure trove of things that have fallen on the ground, like branches, cones, dead straws or dry plants. Blend these with soft clay to create fun sculptures!

If you don't have soft clay, you can make your own play dough.

No-Cook Play Dough Recipe:

4 cups plain flour (all purpose)

4 tablespoons vegetable oil

1 cup salt

4 tablespoons cream of tartar

Up to 3 cups boiling water (adding in increments until it feels just right)

Food coloring (optional)

Mix the flour, salt, cream of tartar and oil in a large mixing bowl.

Add boiling water and stir continuously until it becomes a sticky, combined dough. If you want, you can add food coloring to the dough. After allowing it to cool down, take it out of the bowl and knead it well for a couple of minutes until all of the stickiness has gone. This is very important so don't stop until you are happy with the texture. If it stays sticky, add a touch more flour until it's just right.

Arts and Crafts
Winter

We all know how much fun it is to make snow angels. You can even make it more fun by decorating your snow angel with a mosaic of birdseed to delight your feathered friends.

Studying snowflakes is very interesting, but also hard as they melt very quickly. You need a magnifying glass and a dark cloth you have stored in the freezer. When it snows, lay your cloth on the ground and allow snowflakes to land on the fabric. Before they melt look through the magnifying glass to see the different sizes and shapes of each snowflake. You might discover that like people, no two snowflakes are alike.

Frozen Sun Catchers are very beautiful and easy to make. All you need is a bowl or can made of aluminum or plastic. Fill each bowl half full with water and drop objects you like into it. Place string or yarn in the bowl, leaving a loop on top for hanging. Put each bowl or can in the freezer or them leave outside overnight. When frozen, pull the sun catcher and hang it outdoors. It's beautiful to watch the sun shine through your sun catcher. This might be a great opportunity to talk about what will need to happen to make it to melt. Your discussion might lead you to the topic of global warming.

Bring paper, a pencil and a magnifying glass out in the snow and look for bird footprints. Look at the footprints through your magnifying glass and make a sketch. Take it home and try to find out what kind of bird made the footprints.

Organic and Sustainable Farming

Organic farming means that the farmer grows his food without using chemicals in the soil to make them grow faster. Instead, he uses plant and animal waste. In the old days, before chemical fertilizers had been invented, that's how farmers grew their food. They didn't call it organic food then, it was just food.

The sustainable farmer often grows organic food. But, his priority is to cultivate the land without damaging it. He's always thinking about balance: taking no more than the earth can give, and giving back what he can.

Activity!

Make yourself an organic fruit salad for lunch. Combine frozen blueberries, raspberries, cherries and mangos in a re-usable container, and the fruit will thaw out by lunchtime. You can drizzle a bit of maple syrup over the salad for some added delicious sweetness. Or, pack a yogurt in your lunchbox!

Biodiversity is the system by which all the earth's creatures live together. In their myriad of ways, all these creatures contribute to keeping the system healthy and alive. The loss of biodiversity is one of the greatest challenges we face on this planet!

Did you know?

That to make a tablespoon of honey you need 2000 flowers and twelve very busy bees?

Did you know?

That sustainable farming encourages biodiversity? Many sustainable farmers plant grass buffers along their field borders. They provide food and shelter for animals. There's a greater variety of plant and animal life surrounding sustainable farms, than compared to conventional farms because sustainability means you don't take more space for fields than what is necessary.

Activity!

When you're in your backyard, in the park, or out in the forest, look around and think about what part of the landscape harbours the greatest biodiversity! Research what you can do to support biodiversity in your backyard!

Compost

Organic and sustainable farmers will use compost and other natural methods of fertilization. Composting is when the farmer saves all the organic waste from his farm so that it can break down naturally with the help of worms and other microbes and make natural fertilizer for his fields. It's powerful stuff!

Activity!

If you want to try your hand at composting you might start by collecting a few things that you think might work for your compost. If you have access to a patch of soil, try burying them. Check regularly to see how quickly they decompose!

Bring nature into your home with a terrarium. All you need it a bit of gravel, soil, moss, seeds or small plants, and glass jars. Plant herb seeds, or choose a plant you find interesting in shape and color. Add colorful stones on top of the soil.

You don't have to be a farmer to compost. Composts could be kept in backyards, on porches and balconies, even in your own kitchen!

Most of us love chocolate! Unfortunately a lot of our chocolate is grown in a way that is not sustainable. Rain forests are cleared, pesticides with harmful chemicals are used, and field workers often don't get paid a fair wage. One way to change this is to look for chocolate made from shade-grown cacao. Another way is to look for the label 'fair trade'. This means that the cacao farmer receives a fair price for his chocolate, enough to sustain him, his family, his workers and his farm.

Much of the world's population earns a living from selling its products and labor.

In poorer countries, a lot of people have to sell their goods and services at a price that isn't fair for the amount of effort that went into the work. They work very hard and receive only a tiny bit of what is due to them.

Fair-trade is a simple concept. It's about paying the people who produce the goods and services you buy, a fairer price for their efforts. It is a price that respects their contribution, and allows them to sustain themselves and their families in a dignified manner.

Protecting Our Soil

When you're out and about,
pay attention to the soil beneath your feet.
Compare soil found in the park with the soil you find
on the beach or in the forest. You might start a journal
to record your observations. Or compare different
types of soil from season to season. You can create
your journal from brown paper bags. Use at least four
halves of a paper bag, a hole puncher, string and
paint or crayons to decorate
the cover.

The sustainable farmer takes care of his land by rotating his crops. One year he might plant cabbage, and the next year he might choose to plant corn. Another year he might let his field rest. This way he makes sure his field gets many nutrients from diverse crops and gets plenty of rest from the hard work of providing us food. He values the earth and respects it for its generosity and boundless gifts. He does not demand what the earth cannot produce.

If you're itching to try your hand at gardening and don't have a backyard, find out if there's a community garden in your neighbourhood! Or, you could make a container garden on your fire escape! Or plant a few seeds in a window box and research ways to keep your soil healthy!

Did you know?

That it can take the earth 500 to 1,000 years to produce a single inch of topsoil? It's very important that we protect our topsoil!

Earthworms are VIPs when it comes to topsoil! They make tunnels that allow more air and water to penetrate the ground. And they bring subsoil to the surface to be fertilized. A single earthworm can digest 36 tons of subsoil in one year!

Certain bugs love eating our crops and would happily finish all our food before it gets to us. The sustainable farmer might allow some bugs like praying mantises to devour the bugs that eat his food, or he might plant crops the bugs don't like next to the crops the bugs do like. This prevents the bugs from getting too close. Planting hedges next to fields also prevents the wind from blowing away topsoil. The farmer knows that protecting his topsoil is important because it's the most nutrient rich layer of soil on the earth's surface.

Container Garden

Everyone could enjoy growing food! Gardening is a great way for families to learn new skills and have fun. When you care for your own plants, you learn about the science of plants, animals, the weather, environment, and about eating healthy!

Whether you want to grow food in a garden, on your balcony, in a window box or at a community garden, you can start here!

Container gardens are great because they don't require that much space. Your garden can be the size of a few jars to several large pots. The size makes it manageable for new gardeners. You don't need a big garden to enjoy your own green space!

You can aim for a variety of outcomes for your garden:

Keep it simple!

First, make a list of what you are interested in growing. You might want to grow some edible plants, beautiful flowers or herbs. Don't start with too many things; it is easy to add more at a later time.

You can transplant seedlings from your local nursery, but you can also start from seeds! Remember to read the instructions on the seedling or seed pack first. They will tell you everything you need to know about the amount of sun, water and space the plant will need.

Here are some plants that grow very well in containers:

tomatoes, lettuce, spinach, radishes, green onions, strawberries, carrots, cucumbers, and green beans.

Herbs also grow easily in containers. For your herb garden, you might want to start with basil, parsley, oregano, rosemary, cilantro, chives or thyme.

Try growing fascinating plants like corn, pumpkins, strawberries, sunflowers and tomatoes.

Plant flowers that attract butterflies, ladybugs and other interesting insects or birds.

You could also try to grow plants that appeal to all senses:

Touch – woolly lamb's ear, aloe vera, Jerusalem sage, and snapdragons.

Taste – mint, wild strawberries, rosemary, carrots, cherry tomatoes.

Smell – jasmine, sweet peas, lavender, pelargonium, chocolate cosmos, and lemon balm.

Sight – daffodils, rainbow chard, marigolds, chameleon plant, sunflowers.

Sound – love-in-a-mist, corn, bamboo, greater quaking grass. They make lovely rustling sounds in the wind.

Watch Your Garden Grow

Materials you will need:

1. Organic potting soil mixed with all-natural organic fertilizer.
2. Seedlings or seeds of your choice.
3. Planting container/s of choice.
4. Small gardening shovel.

Choose an area or a window with the most hours of direct sunlight each day.

Tip!

Containers don't have to be regular pots. You can repurpose wooden crates or use the bottom half of milk cartons as planters. Just make sure the container has holes at the bottom to allow for fast draining, which herbs prefer.

Note: While being creative about containers, try to avoid using plastic ones, as it might leak chemicals to your soil when it heats up in the sun.

Use a trellis or teepee to grow beans or sweet peas.

Tip!

Where to get help? You could look for advice from community or local gardening groups.

Activity!

Chart the progress of your garden. Use math to measure your plant's growth with a ruler, count new strawberries, shoots and leaves.

Keep a magnifying glass handy so that you could examine and inspect your plant, both for fun and to see if the plant is healthy.

Use plants as models for drawings, and then color your drawings with leaves from your plants (leaf rubbing).

Make a list of things you want to discover about your garden; why are weeds considered a pest? What is the definition of an insect?

To start the seedlings, you could use:

plant pots

egg cartons

egg shells

toilet paper rolls

paper cups

cut off bottom of a box

juice boxes

waxed milk or cream containers

Did you know?

According to the Guinness Book of World Records, the tallest sunflower grew to 25 and a half feet high. That is about as high as four men standing on each other's heads!

Carrots actually come in a range of colors! White and yellow carrots come from Europe, and purple carrots come from the Middle East. Orange carrots are a fairly recent invention, created by crossing various other colors.

REMEMBER: Starting to grow plants can be a challenge, and all gardeners make mistakes that they learn from. Gardening involves ups and downs, but you will learn as you go. Your garden will get better with time, year after year. Who knows, you might even develop a green thumb!

Activities around your container garden!

Watering

Digging

Planting vegetables, fruits and flowers in the right seasons

Picking flowers

Cutting herbs, picking vegetables and fruits when they are ripe and ready to eat

Using food from you garden to prepare healthy food, such as salads for school lunches

Craft activities using harvested seeds, plants and flowers

Composting

Weeding

Preparing the soil with organic fertilizer

Gathering seeds and dried flowers

Replanting and re-potting.

Eat Locally

It's good to know where the food on our plate comes from, and it's also good to know that it was grown by someone who cares about the environment. If there are organic and sustainable farms in the vicinity of your town or city, you might want to take a drive and have a look at what they're doing.

By purchasing local foods in-season, you reduce emissions caused by shipping foods thousands of miles. Also, your food dollars go directly to the farmer, and your family will be able to enjoy the health benefits of eating fresh, unprocessed fruits and vegetables. Buying seasonal produce also pro-

vides an exciting opportunity to try new foods and to experiment with seasonal recipes.

Sometimes produce from local farms are a bit more expensive than produce from large-scale farms that are located further away. But it's worthwhile to buy local produce for many reasons. First, we know that not much energy has gone into transporting the produce to market. Second, we know where the food is coming from. And third, we're helping small-scale local farmers stay in business!

Did you know?

- A conventional carrot travels 1,838 miles to reach your dinner table.

- 'Food miles' is the distance your food travels to get to your table. Food miles add up as countries export and import foods. Often, countries export and import the same type of food. Now that just doesn't sound right! If a type of food is grown locally in the area, why export it to another area, only to import the same type of food?

- Local foods require less packaging because they don't have to travel long distances.

- Local, sustainable farms can produce greater varieties of fruits and vegetables than large, industrial farms. Small farms protect our heritage by passing down 'heirloom' varieties carefully cultivated through the centuries.

Eating Seasonally

Eating locally also means eating seasonally. It means that we only eat fruits and vegetables that are in season in our geographical area. For those of us who live in the north, this means we get to enjoy our fruits and vegetables in late summer and fall and root vegetables in early winter. For those of us living in more southern climates, eating seasonally offers a greater variety of fruits and vegetables throughout the year.

Harvest time is a great opportunity for the whole family to buy fruits and vegetables in bulk at local farm stands or farmers' markets. These can be enjoyed in their fresh, great-tasting state, or can be canned and preserved to let the taste of summer last long into the winter.

Easy applesauce

Peel and quarter your apples. Cut into small chunks, place in a saucepan and pour enough water to barely cover the apples. Squeeze a bit of lemon juice and as much raw sugar as you would like, but not too much. Simmer for about 20 minutes on low heat. When cooled, mash up your sauce with a fork and pour into your sterilized glass jar. All done!

Your own Popsicle shop!

Make your own sweet popsicles from fruits and juices. You don't need to add any sugar! Slice peeled raspberries into rounds with a lollipop stick in each one and freeze, then dip into dark chocolate on one side and quickly pop back into the freezer! You don't even need to have molds, paper cups will do. For a birthday party you can make popsicles with strawberries, yogurt, shortcake and vanilla! When you make fresh fruit popsicles, fresh mint can add to the freshness!

Why is eating seasonally better for our environment?

Locally grown fruits and vegetables are delicious. Ask your grocer which ones are in season.

Well, pretty much for the same reason as eating locally: it reduces the toll that transportation takes on the earth's resources and it supports our local community. And it means that we always get our vegetables and fruits when they are fresh and less expensive because they haven't had to travel a long distance.

Besides, whenever one ingredient goes out of season, you can be sure that another delicious food is on its way back into season to tempt us all!

Eating seasonally helps us reconnect with nature's cycles and the passing of time!

Mickey's Seed Crackers

1 cup sesame seeds

1 cup linseeds/flaxseeds

$^1/_2$ cup pumpkin seeds

$^1/_2$ cup sunflower oil

$^1/_2$ cup egg whites / almost 3 egg whites

$^3/_4$ cup boiling hot water

$^1/_2$ tbsp sea salt

Mix and stir ingredients together and let rest for 20 minutes. Pour the dough onto a sheet of baking paper. The dough should be rather wet. Spread the dough onto an oven tray until it's as thin as a cracker. Bake in the oven at 250° F for 60-90 minutes, or until very crisp. Cut the bread immediately with a pizza slicer.

Enjoy with delicious toppings!

What a journey it Has Been!

We hope that you have enjoyed exploring the brave new world of green living with your friends and family. Perhaps you have already taken steps on the road toward a sustainable lifestyle. If so, congratulations! You're helping to keep our planet healthy and balanced for a long time to come. If you've seen that there is more work to do, we still congratulate you! You've already taken an important step by reading this book! We're all in this journey together and we all have our work cut out for us. So long as we keep an open mind, stay curious and eager to learn, there's great hope for a green future for this earth.

We're so lucky that our planet exists! We're lucky that it finds itself at a perfect distance from the sun to create conditions for life. It's simply wondrous that our planet should foster and shelter the intricate eco-system that holds our lives together.

Since we are the top dog in the life chain, it is our responsibility to preserve it in all its myriad forms. We can only do that when we have become aware of our environment and understand how fragile it is. We can't allow actions we take for granted in our daily lives to have tragic repercussions in distant places, and even result in the extinction of plant or animal species. On the road to going green, we have to stand firm on the side of our environment. We can't make compromises!

all human beings, all over the planet. If we embody those values in our lives, others will do the same and the quality of all our lives will improve. We hope that this book has given you a chance to think about what constitutes your well-being and what your values are. Perhaps you've even had a chance to rethink them!

Perhaps you traveled through this book with your family to learn together. When families cooperate, many good things happen. The activities and tips you found throughout this book could be enjoyed by all the generations in your family.

Keep learning with your friends and family, talk about the choices you make and be a model for others. Stay positive, stay optimistic!

We can still turn things around if we all make green our color! GO GREEN!

Until next time!

You have read that going green doesn't just involve the 'Three R's' or buying organic and sustainable food. It's a way of life that goes much deeper than that. It begins when we follow the values that are intrinsic to a healthy and happy life for

References

Adams, W. M. (2006). The future of sustainability: Re-thinking environment and development in the twenty-first century. The World Conservation Union.

Bell, S. & Morse, S. (2008). Sustainability indicators: Measuring the immeasurable? UK: Earthscan,

Breiting, S., Mayer, M., & Mogensen, F. (2005). Quality criteria for ESD schools: Guidelines to enhance the quality of education for sustainable development

Butler, S.D. (2008). Environmental change, injustice and sustainability. Bioethical inquiry, 5, 11–19

Day, H., & Jankey, S. G (1996). Lessons from the literature. Towards a holistic model of quality of life. In Renwick, R., Brown, I., & Nagler, M. (eds.), Quality of life in health promotion and rehabilitation. Conceptual approaches, issues and applications, (pp. 39-50). Thousand Oaks: Sage.

Dodds, S. (1997). Toward a science of "sustainability": Improving the way ecological economics understands human well-being. Ecological economics, 23, 95-111.

Felce, D., & Perry, J. (1996) Assessment of quality of life. In Schalock, R. L. (ed.), Quality of life. Volume I: Conceptualisation and measurement (pp.63-72). Washington, DC: American Association on mental retardation.

Griggs, D. (2013). Rethinking sustainable development in the anthropocene. From: http://anthropocenejournal.com/2013/03/24/rethinking-sustainable-development-intheanthropocene/

Gruenewald, D. A. (2003). The best of both worlds. A critical pedagogy of place, Educational researcher, 32(A), 3-12.

Jónsdóttir, Á. (2013). Making values visible: A photographic exploration of sustainable living.

Keith, K. D. (2004). International quality of life: Current conceptual, measurement, and implementation issues. From: http://www.sciencedirect.com/science/article/pii/S0074775001800057

Kozak, S., & Elliot, S. (2011). Connecting the dots: Key learning strategies for environmental education, citizenship, and sustainability. Learning for a sustainable future.

Orr, D. W. (2002). Four challenges of sustainability. Conservation Biology, 16 (6), 1457-1460.

Schalock, R. L. (1996). Reconsidering the conceptualisation and measurement of quality of life. In Schalock, Robert L. (ed.), Quality of life, conceptualization and measurement, 1, 77-87.

Sterling, S. (2009). Sustainable education: Re-visioning learning and change. UK: Green books.

UNESCO (n.d.). Educating for a sustainable future

www.aza.org

www.nooa.gov

www.disneyfriendsforchange.com

www.naturerocks.org

www.epa.gov/climatechange/science/causes.html

www.childrenandnature.org

www.epa.vic.gov.au

www.thecarbonaccount.com

meetthegreens.pbskids.org

www.naturalinquirer.org

www.epa.gov

education.nationalgeographic.com

www.nature.org

www.neok12.com

kidshealth.org

earthday.org

www.kidsgardening.org

environment.nationalgeographic.com/environment/global-warming/solar-power-profile/

www.esta-uk.net

shrinkthatfootprint.com